THE COLLATERAL EFFECT OF SUCCESS

How to Escape from Frustration
and Reclaim a Life of Fulfillment

Dani Ferrara

Dani Ferrara Transformational Coach

Copyright © 2021 Dani Ferrara

All rights reserved

The characters and events portrayed in this book are fictitious. Any similarity to real persons, living or dead, is coincidental and not intended by the author.

No part of this book may be reproduced, or stored in a retrieval system, or transmitted in any form or by any means, electronic, mechanical, photocopying, recording, or otherwise, without express written permission of the publisher.

Cover design by: Dani Ferrara

True happiness is not an unattainable dream.

The answer lies in genuine love and dedication to a purpose bigger than yourself.

There is such power in them that it staggers the imagination!

"This is the true joy in life, the being used for a purpose recognized by yourself as a mighty one, the being a force of nature instead of a feverish selfish little clod of ailments and grievances complaining that the world will not devote itself to making me happy.

I am of the opinion that my life belongs to the whole community and, as long as I live, it is my privilege to do for it whatever I can.

I want to be thoroughly used up when I die, for the harder I work the more I live.

I rejoice in life for its own sake.

Life is no brief candle to me.

It is a sort of splendid torch which I've got to hold up for the moment and I want to make it burn as brightly as possible before handing it on to future generations."

GEORGE BERNARD SHAW

CONTENTS

Title Page

Copyright

Dedication

Epigraph

My Mission

"NOTHING INSPIRES ME ANYMORE"	1
"WHY SHOULD I CARE?"	3
HIGH RISK OF SUICIDE	5
WATCH OUT FOR THE DEAD-ENDS: REGRETS	8
ARE YOU PLAYING THE 'RIGHT GAME'?	12
WHY DOES LIFE SEEM SO COMPLICATED?	14
LIFE IS LIKE A HUGE VIDEO GAME	16
THE CALL OF DUTY	18
ACTIVATING YOUR VIRTUAL REALITY GLASSES	20
THE INNER GAME	23
"CHANGE IS DIFFICULT"	26
REDUCING THE PRESSURE AND STRESS FROM	28

THE GAME

TRANSFORMING CONFLICTS INTO GIFTS 30

TRANSFORMING CHALLENGES INTO GROWING OPPORTUNITIES 34

TRANSFORMING THE GAME OF FETCH INTO THE GAME OF STILLNESS 37

TRANSFORMING FLEETING CONTENTMENT INTO LONG-LASTING FELICITY 42

RECLAIMING YOUR AUTHENTICITY 46

THE GAME PARADOX 49

WHAT IF YOU TURNED THIS GAME AROUND? 53

THE POWER OF THE TRANSFORMATIONAL COACHING TO BOOST YOUR GAME AND CREATE THE LIFE YOU DESIRE 56

COACHING IS ABOUT THRIVING! 59

MEET JOHN: A 49-YEAR-OLD AMBITIOUS ENTREPRENEUR 62

'ZOMBIE' STATE: HOW LONG ARE GOING TO REMAIN DEAD INSIDE? 68

MEMENTO MORI EXERCISE: TAKING THE HEADSTONE TEST 72

EXPERIENCING THE "ECSTASY OF AN INSPIRED LIFE" 75

About The Author 77

MY MISSION

Alluding to George Bernard Shaw's quote:

My mission is to ignite your light shine as brightly as possible as you can be more present for yourself and your loved ones and keep pursuing new adventures that allow you to express your unique talents in profound service to the world. Thus, celebrating a lifetime of true joy and fulfillment.

"NOTHING INSPIRES ME ANYMORE"

"I don't even recognize myself"

"I feel lonely and completely disconnected from my family"

Sounds familiar?

That's not so uncommon.

Although Americans are earning more, they are stuck on a treadmill thinking they'd be content if they just had a little more money.

But when they get it, they discover something else they want.

Because they're never satisfied with what they have. They can never have enough, according to the U.S. Census Bureau.

You have been told since you were a child that wealth brings peace of mind and happiness, but it turns out your grandfather was right:

Money can help you achieve your objectives and provide for your future though it doesn't guarantee fulfillment.

"WHY SHOULD I CARE?"

When your personal significance is threatened, you react with fight or flight responses, for example:

- Displays of superiority, like harnessing status symbols;

- Displays of power, like aggressive attempts to control or manipulate others;

- Social withdrawal.

The inevitable result of the Conventional Success mind frame, which focuses on wealth, respect, fame, popularity, and profit are insulation, shame, guilt, and frustration.

HIGH RISK OF SUICIDE

In "Why People Die by Suicide" Thomas Joiner describes how intense emotional pain often comes from a perceived lack of belonging.

"To be lonely is to feel unwanted and unloved, and therefore unlovable.

Loneliness is a taste of death."

On the other side, when your sense of significance is accomplished, your well-being, sense of identity, and interpersonal connection levels bloom.

It's from here our conversation begins:

Life might seem normal and functional: As a businessman, you live striving to check goals off the list and strive to do more, but you feel in your bones:

YOU ARE MEANT FOR SOMETHING BIGGER.

Perhaps the fear of change tries to convince you that you are happy, saying you don't need anything other than what you already have, though YOU KNOW that success comes at a price.

You feel that living can be much more exciting, but you have no clue how to make it different: Things you considered valuable before once you zoom out, you realize now some of those "amazing moments" were not so meaningful.

Or, maybe you just move on and hope to wake up happier magically, never doing anything concrete about it...

Then, what is costing you to stay where you are?

As a leader, what legacy do you want to leave in people's lives, and what's the impact you want to create in the world?

How do you want to be remembered by your family when you are not here anymore?

WATCH OUT FOR THE DEAD-ENDS: REGRETS

"Let us prepare our minds as if we'd come to the very end of life. Let us postpone nothing. Let us balance life's books each day. The one who puts the finishing touches on their life each day is never short of time."

SENECA

Both Roman Emperor Marcus Aurelius and Steve Jobs pointed to contemplating death as an exceptional form to stimulate more purposeful living.

Despite being one of the most influential men of his time, the Emperor would keep his mortality in evidence every single day: Aurelius had a personal journal in which he registered those contemplations:

> *"You could leave life right now. Let that determine what you do and say and think."*

While it might sound morbid, internalizing death as an inevitable event is an effective medicine to some poisons of the modern world like selfishness, greed, and lack of tolerance.

Jobs says that remembering that we'll be dead soon is a powerful tool when making big choices in life:

> *"Because almost everything - all external expectations, all pride, all fear of embarrassment or failure - these things just fall away in the face of death, leaving only what is truly important."*

A nurse called Bronnie Ware authored an article called "Regrets of the Dying", about people's regrets on their deathbeds, and these below were the most frequent ones:

"I wish I hadn't worked so hard"

"I wish I'd dared to live true to myself, rather than doing what others expected of me"

"I wish I'd had the courage to express my feelings"

"I wish I had stayed in touch with my friends"

"I wish I had let myself be happier"

The first one, *"I wish I hadn't worked so hard"*, came from EVERY male patient she nursed: *"They missed their children's youth and their partner's companionship."*

If there was a movie about your story would you want to watch it?

If NOT, it's not too late to TURN THIS GAME AROUND and find appreciation, joy, peace, and love for everything that is here now but won't be here forever.

> *"Death is not the greatest loss in life. The greatest loss is what dies inside us while we live."*

NORMAN COUSINS

ARE YOU PLAYING THE 'RIGHT GAME'?

The RIGHT game where you meet the RIGHT girl, get married, have the RIGHT kids, put them in the RIGHT universities, and make the RIGHT amount of money, IS NOT NECESSARILY the game of fulfillment.

Yes, it's the game played in our culture, in which THE ONLY WAY you'll ever be accomplished and exultant is when you achieve those things.

This concept reminds me of a story about a millionaire who has been named Time Magazine's Man of the Year.

He said he went home after work and planned to kill himself since he'd realized every single desire in his journey just hadn't experienced the satisfaction he was expecting.

He got a new lease on life, having realized that he was living a false paradigm.

WHY DOES LIFE SEEM SO COMPLICATED?

You've accumulated thousands of contradictory beliefs during your lifetime, resulting in a constant internal conflict.

Those concepts are like hallucinations foggy:

It's not easy to disperse it since you don't want to step outside your comfort zone. But when you are willing to remove it, you see it's worthwhile.

WITHOUT THE FOGGY, THINGS GET INCREDIBLY CLEAR — NONE OF THE OPTIONS IS HIDDEN — IT'S A FEARLESS STATE OF BEING: THERE'S NO LIMIT TO IT!

When I lived like a zombie all I wanted was to have a fairy godmother to spark some clarity of mind and heart.

Here's what I learned:

LIFE IS LIKE A HUGE VIDEO GAME

The game's objective is to evolve and be more tolerant, kind, and empathetic towards the other players.

Each of us has come to this world to work on our mission: we accomplish it by sharing and participating in experiences with other players.

Frequently, rather than getting on with our game, we try to interfere with other players' games. Plus instead of LEARNING from them, we try to CHANGE them, for example:

"People should be nicer."

"Kids must be well-behaved."

"My wife should agree with me."

THE CALL OF DUTY

"The true man is revealed in difficult times. So when trouble comes, think of yourself as a wrestler whom God, like a trainer, has paired with a tough young buck.

For what purpose? To turn you into Olympic-class material. No one's difficulties ever gave him a better test than yours, if you are prepared to make use of them the way a wrestler makes use of an opponent in peak condition."

EPICTETUS

The best games propel you to keep improving and enable you to collaborate with other players. You're not upset if the game gets difficult.

You WANT it to get harder. You're having fun and celebrating it. It's exciting because you see that you are evolving:

You understand that the challenges are part of the game, functioning as algorithms to improve our skills.

> *"What would have become of Hercules, do you think, if there had been no lion, hydra, stag or boar? — and no savage criminals to rid the world of?"*
>
> EPICTETUS

ACTIVATING YOUR VIRTUAL REALITY GLASSES

Yes, this video game comes with virtual reality glasses. However, few people know about it or, if they know it, cannot use it properly.

I know it seems SUPER PREPOSTEROUS and a bit suspicious: "ok, I'm living in the feeling of my thinking, unless something bad happens."

THE COLLATERAL EFFECT OF SUCCESS

Not exactly.

For example: If you are in your office where your desk is piled high with a bunch of work, you had a turbulent meeting, and like, there's no reason for you to be content, but you are.

Why?

Because in your desk drawer, there are two tickets to Paris and you know that tomorrow morning, regardless of what's around you, you will be on vacation.

The opposite would be true.

Let's say you're in Paris, walking through Champs-Élysées. Suddenly, you see a plane fly overhead, and you instantly become depressed.

Why?

Because the plane reminds you of your work: your vocations are about to end.

When you are in love, you are constantly

over the moon. Things happen on a stressful day where you go to your stressful job and have a stressful conversation - You feel FANTASTIC, though.

And a good day is where you can take some time off work, and you get to hang out with your friends or your loved ones.

On the other hand, there are many times that 'this good day' doesn't make you feel 'FANTASTIC' - You are unmotivated, though.

It still matters what your wife does.

It still matters what's happening out there in the world.

In other words: you live the reality that you project with your thoughts.

THE INNER GAME

"To know thyself is the beginning of wisdom"

SOCRATES

The more you explore your thoughts and feelings, the better you are at adapting to change. It helps you to keep evolving and handle problems with more objectivity.

Socrates also says that what separates humans from mere brutes is our capacity of transcending the instinct and desire to make conscious and ethical choices by thinking before acting.

We all know how tough the routine is and how things can get a little bit chaotic.

However, it is easier to blame other people or circumstances around you and say: 'Oh, I misbehaved because I was carried away by the heat of the moment.'

Although you cannot control other people's responses, your reaction is 100% in your hands.

You can master your nature and increase self-control if you are willing to dive deep into your deepest secrets.

The renowned scientist Sir Isaac Newton lost all his savings and got reduced to near poverty after being scammed by John Blunt, the initiator of the infamous South Sea Bubble of 1720.

In the aftermath of this terrible event, Newton stated: "Although I can calculate the motions of heavenly bodies, I cannot understand the madness of men."

Sir Isaac was an expert in the motions of planets; However, he didn't fathom the closest thing to him — HIMSELF.

> *"The more challenging or threatening the situation or context to be assimilated and affirmed, the greater the stature of the person who can achieve it. The demon that you can swallow gives you its power, and the greater life's pain, the greater life's reply."*
>
> JOSEPH CAMPBELL

"CHANGE IS DIFFICULT"

What makes change seem unpleasant is the fact you want to force it without building an internal basis previously.

For example, imagine for a moment that you hit traffic every single day driving to work.

If you discovered a shortcut to get there or a viable and affordable way of teleportation, how many times would I have to show the new option to you?

The entire transformation experience is simplified if motivated by broadening your perspective for the benefits of the new scenario:

> *"At the moment you decide that what you know is more important than what you have been taught to believe, you will have shifted gears in your quest for abundance."*
>
> RALPH WALDO EMERSON

REDUCING THE PRESSURE AND STRESS FROM THE GAME

I f you feel that tension is taking a toll on your well-being the 'optimism applied' - the constant positive attitude REVOLUTIONIZES YOUR RELATIONSHIPS AND GRANTS YOU MORE PEACE OF MIND.

Optimistic people are more resilient and

HAPPIER because they can see alternatives and growing opportunities in challenging situations - **they don't panic or get overwhelmed.**

Since you have so much on your plate it can be difficult to internalize this mindset.

However, when you handle a problem facing it as a temporary inconvenience or working to solve it without being alarmed, you save a lot of energy: **it explains why optimistic people live six to eight years longer than average.**

Negative emotions, on the other hand, can damage your inner peace, especially if you keep ruminating about what 'could have been' - **The effects of 'chronic pessimism' are like smoking two packs of cigarettes a day.**

The most effective way to assimilate this idea is carefully thinking through the entire situation, like in the examples below:

TRANSFORMING CONFLICTS INTO GIFTS

It's complex to be running a business, be a parent and be in a relationship. Mixing those three, and you're in a perfect storm!

We tend to become quite susceptible to those 'storms' - Thus, we go from a moment of tranquility to a moment of hardship - a perfect scenario to silly conflicts.

Although it's a foolish example, the story below illustrates well the point:

Your wife wants to go to the nearby Italian restaurant.

And your position is:

"I want to go far from here, in a Chinese restaurant."

"What's wrong with you?"

"We should do this; my idea is much interesting than yours."

The objective is to go deeper into each other's reason and use empathy as a guide:

"I am looking for a quiet place to talk. I have missed talking to you.

We haven't had a chance to sit down and take time to hear each other out and see what's happening. That's why I want to go to the Italian restaurant."

And you go:

"But the Chinese one is closer. I have a super important project tomorrow and I want to make sure the dinner doesn't take any longer."

Now you have gone to the underlying deeper reasons for your positions, then you can let go of those positions and ask:

"Is there a new position that somehow satisfies both?"

In other words, profound rejoice is interconnected with **REVERBERATING LOVE AND GIVING THE BEST OF YOU**, being hand in hand with:

- Living wisely and virtuously by demonstrating bravery and moderation, and overcoming what Stoics called the "unhealthy passions" that interfere with your ability to live in accord with wisdom and justice;

- Being authentic and expressing to your fullest potential;

- Striving to progress even more — remaining far from your comfort zone;

- Fostering empathy and kindness

You can convert those situations into small gifts to strengthen your relationships through kindness and empathy rather than being rude and focusing only on your needs, which cause distance and erode trust.

TRANSFORMING CHALLENGES INTO GROWING OPPORTUNITIES

By overcoming difficulties without losing composure, YOU AVOID A LOT OF STRESS AND SAVE YOUR PRECIOUS TIME considering you will focus on WHAT MATTERS in these situations:

CREATING SOLUTIONS!

If instead of:

"I wish I hadn't lost my job"

You thought:

"I lost my job; what intelligent solution can I find right now?"

Whenever you get to a positive or negative conclusion, make sure you're aware of all the elements of the situation.

Besides, it is helpful to reflect:

- How will it feel in a week or 5 years?

- What are some other aspects you will learn from this problem for the long term?

- Which mind frame are you gonna invest in the future if you want to save your valuable energy?

Scenario 1: You are doing your best and it would be sensational to accomplish X.

If the contrary occurs, Y, you'll be miserable.

So, you will feel stressed since the beginning of it considering you can't assure that you'll achieve X.

Scenario 2: You are doing your best and it would be sensational to accomplish X.

Still, if Y occurs, you won't overreact.

Instead, you'll remain serene and transform the outcome into a gift and opportunity to grow.

So nothing to stress about. Either case will be good.

TRANSFORMING THE GAME OF FETCH INTO THE GAME OF STILLNESS

"It is good to have an end to journey toward; but it is the journey that matters, in the end."

ERNEST HEMINGWAY

Being obsessed with your dreams is like playing a game of fetch with yourself, using them as the bone.

There's nowhere for you to get to—you're just here.

Presence is not just about the hours you spend with people:

THE MOST IMPORTANT IS HOW YOU DO IT.

When you tell your wife: *"I love you"*, but you're not feeling the love, and you're not even looking at her or you're out the door, it doesn't have any impact.

Whereas, if you are present, looking your wife in the eye, you can FEEL THE LOVE IN YOUR HEART.

As you're declaring to her, it took ten seconds, and it can shake her to the bone.

If you spend the whole weekend with your family distracted, you haven't made any connection.

It's about the QUALITY OF THE TIME, NOT QUANTITY.

> *"If you are perpetually angry, depressed, confused, and unloving, or your attention is elsewhere, it won't matter how successful you become or who is in your life — you won't enjoy any of it.*

> *Most of us spend our time seeking happiness and security without acknowledging the underlying purpose of our search.*

> *Each of us is looking for a path back to the present. We are trying to find good enough reasons to be satisfied now.*

> *How we pay attention to the present moment largely determines the character of our experience and, therefore, the quality of our lives."*
>
> SAM HARRIS

Thus, it's indispensable to cherish the journey, rather than focusing exclusively on the result:

When you stop running your days on automatic pilot, you strengthen your relationships, mainly with loved ones.

For 75 years, Harvard University monitored the physical and emotional health of 724 people. This project began when the research subjects were teenagers and followed them into their eighties.

I got astonished by the conclusions of that research project:

The quality of relationships, more than

money or fame, keeps people happy throughout their lives.

Those ties help to delay mental and physical decline and are greater predictors of long and cheerful lives than social class, IQ, or even genes.

I know you may feel exhausted and drained by the pace of your life. Though the energy created when you interact cheerfully with other people is nourishing and healing.

The most significant findings from this study, according to Dr. Waldinger are:

> *"Good relationships keep us happier and healthier. Period."*

> *"Loneliness kills. It's as powerful as smoking or alcoholism."*

How different would your existence be if you slowed down and savored the moments with your loved ones?

TRANSFORMING FLEETING CONTENTMENT INTO LONG-LASTING FELICITY

"Having more money boosts our happiness about life, but it has little if any impact on the daily positive and negative emotions and the uplifts and hassles we experience."

SONJA LYUBOMIRSKY

Purchasing your dream car will give you some satisfaction and excitement. However, the effect won't be as lasting and intense as you might think.

Your contentment curve will flatten quickly, and you'll be driving your 'dream car' without even being aware of it.

Most of the time, you'll realize that all the 'big moments' weren't so significant.

Although they might have shaped your personality and daily routines, they didn't impact the big picture deeply.

When children want a new toy, they'll tell you how bad they want it and swear it's the only toy in the world they'll ever want to play with.

Though once they get the toy, it takes three

days to get bored and look for the next one.

It doesn't mean you won't be enthusiastic about your new car or a milestone you achieved.

Of course, you'll feel great in those moments.

However, your level of excitement won't last for as long as you might've assumed.

If you want to enjoy your money optimally, here are some of Sonja's tips:

- Investing in experiences, developing new abilities, and focusing on interpersonal connections grants your long-lasting moments of satisfaction, like traveling, having dinner in a fancy restaurant with your wife, and getting new hobbies.

- Reverting money into free time to do meaningful stuff makes you feel you are living more intensely, in contrast with being enslaved by work.

- Investing in ANTICIPATION: booking a trip for 3 months from now generates excitement not only during your trip but also during the days before the 'BIG DAY'. It boils down to cherishing the delightful 'looking forward' feeling!

RECLAIMING YOUR AUTHENTICITY

"The final freedom is choosing to live who you are — especially when it's scary, uncertain, inconvenient, or unpopular."

KIM GEORGE

Authenticity is about knowing who you are and what you want DEEPLY, and acting accordingly.

You are open and honest regardless of

people's opinion: YOU KNOW YOU ARE ENOUGH.

People who live authentically embrace their vulnerability and know that what they do is not connected to their self-worth.

As young, you ordinarily disconnect from your original savage grace and creativity in the name of being accepted and liked and not embarrassing yourselves with your peers:

You grow up, try to get jobs and families, and then you form safe and insincere personalities, disconnecting from your courage and inner power.

When you divorce from anything that doesn't get you any acceptance or approval from your environment, you seek the middle.

Not YOUR middle, but the middle of our social groups, and society itself, stripping away your innate creativity.

When you are profoundly aware of who you

are and feel comfortable in your skin, there's no compulsion to control either struggle for external approval: You are finally immune to criticism.

Science has proven that lasting fulfillment is related to discovering your NATURAL STRENGTHS and employing them consistently in service to a noble purpose.

> *"Character is higher than intellect... A great soul will be strong to live, as well as strong to think."*
>
> RALPH WALDO EMERSON

THE GAME PARADOX

"Don't go after happiness; Rather, commit yourself to something bigger than you and let happiness come chasing after you."

VIKTOR FRANKL

"Psychologists who study happiness repeatedly discover a puzzling paradox: the happiest people are those who pay little attention to the goal of becoming happy."

WILLIAM DAMON

Having a noble and special mission empowers you to understand who you are and how you can contribute to the world on a more intentional level.

Without a vision and a purpose, you perish - even your body suffers.

During the Holocaust, someone did a study on the families of concentration camp members. Despite living on very little, if any—no food or water—somehow, they survived.

However, when someone would get news of the passing of the person they were holding onto, they would die in three days like clockwork.

Their vision of what would be like when they got out of the camp was now gone.

A mighty purpose keeps you alive even without food or water and in the most severe living conditions.

Without a strong WHY, there's no way you'll persist through the inevitable storms.

People with a strong purpose do better psychologically and socially.

* So, let's imagine a substance that would:

- Increase your longevity, reduce the risk of heart attack and stroke; cut your risk of Alzheimer's disease by more than half;

- Help you relax during the day and sleep well at night;

- Activate your natural killer cells;

- Diminish your inflammatory cells;

- Increase your good cholesterol and repair your DNA.

Oh, and as a bonus, give you better sex?

It's LIFE PURPOSE. And it's free.

Oh, and the side effects?

More friends.

And did I mention better sex?

* Adapted from *"Life on Purpose: How Living for What Matters Most Changes Everything "*- Victor Strecher

WHAT IF YOU TURNED THIS GAME AROUND?

"Everyone has a purpose, a unique gift or special talent to give to others. And when we blend this unique talent with service to others, we experience the exultation of our own spirit, which is the ultimate goal of goals."

DEEPAK CHOPRA

You can SHY AWAY from seizing the chance of long-held HAPPINESS AND FULFILLMENT, or you can decide you DESERVE MORE:

- What would be like waking up every morning with a limitless reservoir of energy and enthusiasm - Instead of the 'ugh' thought about starting a new day?

- What if you tried to do things that you love like traveling and taking your wife out to a romantic dinner, instead of wasting so much vitality on the treadmill of a work existence?

- How accomplished and cheerful would you be if you honored your dreams, goals, and the desires of your heart?

- How would your wife and children react to your transformation? Would they be turned on, lit up, engaged, and excited in your presence?

- What if you reconnected with your essence to be WHO YOU ARE — rather than letting society define who you are for you?

You received at birth an invitation to show up and live to your fullest potential.

NO EXCLUSIONS.

It's time to listen to the voice inside you that says you're meant for something big because...

{spoiler alert}... YOU ARE!

THE POWER OF THE TRANSFORM-ATIONAL COACHING TO BOOST YOUR GAME AND CREATE THE LIFE YOU DESIRE

"I saw the Angel in the marble, and I carved until I set him free."

MICHELANGELO

C OACHING IS MAGICAL: It's like sculpting a masterpiece inside by carving the detrimental beliefs and fears away.

Soon this stunning work of art experiences such robust freedom generated in consequence of growing (IT'S REALLY MEGA EXCITING!)

You may think: *"I'll hire a coach, and she'll show me what to do."*

Rather, Coaching broadens your horizons through paradigm shifts:

The transformation is powerful because it gives you new eyes, unveiling a whole scenario with solutions and opportunities, creating, consequently, immediate long-term change.

Apart from it, we are working in PARTNERSHIP to CO-DEVELOP a plan with goals and follow-ups during the entire process.

> *"Our chief want in life is somebody who will make us do what we can."*
>
> RALPH WALDO EMERSON

Notice, he said, "CHIEF WANT" and not "one of our many wants."

It's what we want more than anything else:

To find somebody who will make us DO WHAT WE CAN!

A while ago, coaching was only for artists and athletes.

Since the world has become more entrepreneurial and creative, a personal growth movement emerged and the demand for coaches has increased massively.

COACHING IS ABOUT THRIVING!

"I help people discern between things that actually need to be dealt with in the world and those that only seem like problems as part of their individual thought-created realities.

And as they begin to wake up from the dream of thought and start experiencing deeper peace of mind, living gets simpler, and much, much more fun."

MICHAEL NEILL

In my sessions, I provide a safe setting for tackling complex issues and sparkling insights through open and honest communication, with NO JUDGMENT, BUT A LOVING ATTITUDE AND CAREFUL LISTENING.

If you are looking for support to:

- Experience the ECSTASY of living for a PURPOSE that makes you feel UNSTOPPABLE & ALIVE;

- BOOST the relationship with YOURSELF & WITH PEOPLE AROUND YOU, PRINCIPALLY YOUR LOVED ONES;

- RECLAIM your authenticity;

- REGAIN ENTHUSIASM ABOUT LIFE;

- REGULATE YOUR EMOTIONS & STRESS

LEVELS;

- Have CLARITY about: WHO YOU ARE, YOUR STRENGTHS, WHAT ENERGIZES YOU.

.... then look no further!

Let's make it happen and map out a plan to create a gentler, kinder, and more peaceful existence while having even more performance capacity and a richer sense of being alive.

You can get it started by setting your 'TURNING YOUR GAME AROUND CALL':

BECAUSE YOU DESERVE TO INVEST SOME TIME AND ENERGY IN YOUR DREAM LIFE!

IT'S FREE!

https://calendly.com/dani_ferrara

MEET JOHN: A 49-YEAR-OLD AMBITIOUS ENTREPRENEUR

As I took a sip on my morning coffee, I sat staring at my bedroom wall - I kept asking myself:

"How did I get here?"

"What triggered all these events and led me

to a hopeless situation?"

"Was it me?"

"Was it bad luck?"

I was a sales and marketing manager in a multinational company earning six figures. I had a nice car and a spacious house in a quiet suburb. Considering the 'society's measure of success', I was doing well.

I wasn't happy at all, though. Yeah, I was earning good money, but I felt dead inside. I needed to start from scratch a new chapter in my story.

One of my lifelong ambitions was to become an entrepreneur. I've always wanted to start my own virtual business but, every time I tried to move forward, something held me back.

I felt stuck, and I knew it deep down.

I buried myself in a myriad of courses, studying and assimilating everything I could, but I couldn't get any traction.

I even went to a therapist to get help, but it didn't do much. To be honest, I felt caught in a vortex of failure and despair.

I was close to giving up - the situation was beyond me - I felt like a fraud.

Then, out of the blue, a lady called Dani reached out to me. She was inquiring what I do, I sheepishly replied over messenger. Dani detected my lack of focus and confidence right off the bat.

Oh, gosh, another lost opportunity. She knew I was a fraud. She could smell it from a mile away.

Thoughts were swirling in my mind:

"This is never going to work out!"

"I'm going to have to go back to this soul-less job and spend the rest of my days working here, numb and lifeless...."

"I'm not competent, not able to get this done..."

"I'm not good enough…"

"How dare I have the audacity to even try and get started".

To my surprise, she wanted to know more and asked about me in a caring and empathetic way.

I wanted to put up a facade to say to people everything was ok, but I couldn't. So, I decided to only tell her the truth and started revealing what was going on.

Dani listened intently and we had the most empowering chat I have had in years, if not my whole life.

It was like she knew what I was thinking before even saying it:

She read my body language and I knew she was the right person for me to guide me on this journey.

We started coaching together and, two months in, it hit me straight in the face like a hammer blasting a nail.

It was as if a heavy backpack was taken off me as my years of confusion running around in circles seemed all to be leading me to this moment.

This wasn't about setting up a new business: It had everything to do with how I had neglected my well-being for years.

I was self-sabotaging and worse: I had developed an addiction to doing it.

Before moving forward with my business, I had to get in touch with my true essence.

Dani taught me how to observe my thoughts and take responsibility for myself.

I finally shifted out of my victim mindset bit by bit: I stopped using avoidant tactics to not work on my business, I was now able to make conscious decisions on what I needed to prioritize.

Dani also helped me move past my perfectionism, which has allowed me to generate momentum daily.

Other aspects began to improve as well: I'm now able to appreciate being truly present with my family, not making any more excuses: I have much more clarity to make good decisions.

I came to Dani hoping she could help me take the right actions to grow my business.

I got a level of transformation I could never have anticipated, which was far more about me connecting with my true essence and healing old wounds.

'ZOMBIE' STATE: HOW LONG ARE GOING TO REMAIN DEAD INSIDE?

One of the greatest frustrations in a man's life is when his dreams are superior to his results.

When I work with my clients on fulfillment and happiness, I begin with these questions:

"What do you DEEPLY want, and what's in the

way of it right now?"

Not having enough courage is ONLY what is in their way:

"I'm afraid if I took a risk, I would lose my status."

"I'm afraid my wife wouldn't appreciate it if I did this."

It takes courage to ask for help and mold your life THE WAY YOU WANT IT TO BE, but I can assure you the journey towards your fullest potential is EXCITING and REWARDING!

And don't have to settle for less than you can be, share, give or create.

Your FEARS can be real, but the LIMITATIONS YOU SEE ARE NOT.

> *"The pain that's created by avoiding hard work is actually much worse than any pain created from the actual work itself."*

This sharp discomfort is an 'ALARM CLOCK' to awaken you from the 'ZOMBIE MODE' caused by inertia and lack of enthusiasm.

The greatest medicine is you noble purpose since it inspires you to become a better person and allows you to express to your fullest potential, keeping motivation on fire.

PLEASE, TAKE A SECOND and EXAMINE CAREFULLY YOUR LIFE:

If you're not living for a purpose BIGGER THAN YOURSELF that makes you feel UNSTOPPABLE and ALIVE, WHAT ARE YOU WAITING FOR?

How long are you going to remain dead?

Together, we can unlock the magic that is ALREADY inside waiting for the right guidance!

You can get it started by setting your: 'TURNING YOUR GAME AROUND CALL':

https://calendly.com/dani_ferrara

From my heart to yours,

Dani Ferrara

"If the only thing people learned was not to be afraid of their experience, that alone would change the world."

SYD BANKS

MEMENTO MORI EXERCISE: TAKING THE HEADSTONE TEST

"Recently I've been thinking about the difference between the résumé virtues and the eulogy virtues.

The résumé virtues are the ones you list on your résumé and that contribute to external success.

The eulogy virtues are deeper. They're the

virtues that get talked about at your funeral, the ones that exist at the core of your being—whether you are kind, brave, honest or faithful; what kind of relationships you formed.

Most of us have clearer strategies for how to achieve career success than we do for how to develop profound character."

STEPHEN COVEY

The expression MEMENTO MORI, translated from Latin, means 'remember you have to die' and compels you to stop wasting time and reflect on what matters most to you.

Stephen Covey says you need to *"begin with the end"* in mind, considering how you want to be remembered when you're gone.

From this perspective, please draw a headstone, sign your name on it, and write in your date of birth.

For the date of death, write 'TODAY'.

And, then meditate carefully on:

- What would your epitaph be?

- What would your family say about you?

- What would you want people to say about you at your memorial service?

EXPERIENCING THE "ECSTASY OF AN INSPIRED LIFE"

"From Tonight Onwards, Take Complete Control Of Your Life. Decide, Once And For All, To Be The Master Of Your Fate. Run Your Own Race.
Discover Your Calling, And You Will Start To Experience The Ecstasy Of An Inspired Life."

ROBIN SHARMA

ABOUT THE AUTHOR

Dani Ferrara

My name is Dani Ferrara, and I'm an uncompromising Life Coach - Life Purpose Specialist - University of Michigan, devoted to empowering men, just like yourself, who have a lifetime of conventional success, switch off the status quo and make bold moves to create an EPIC LIFE without burning out.

I know EXACTLY what it's like to have a great life outside and, inside, self-doubt - I've been there too.

My journey Until Life Coaching: 'My Why'

I used to travel a lot, long trips twice a year, I had a wonderful job, happy marriage, health...

Since I was a child, I have always dreamed about having EXACTLY that life, but there was something that didn't feel good...

While I tried to handle those feelings, I would just spend my days working and binge-watching on Netflix:

The achievement level was high, but the fulfillment, low.

I felt so disconnected from myself, and living that way was a game of stress and frustration: I was tired of wasting my life in the shadows.

How do I set myself free?

Where had I kept THE REAL DANI?

While I tried to handle those feelings, I would just spend my days working and binge-watching on Netflix:

The achievement level was high, but the fulfillment, low.

I felt so disconnected from myself, and living that way was a game of stress and frustration: I was tired of wasting my life in the shadows.

How do I set myself free?

Where had I kept THE REAL DANI?

Everything changed when I started to pay attention *seriously* to what was happening, instead of numbing myself buying new stuff and watching TV.

Gradually, things became clear in my mind (all the answers we are looking for are inside us):

I felt that I wasn't myself anymore because I wasn´t living to my fullest potential - I was totally 'out of service'.

I was ignoring my purpose in life.

HERE'S WHAT TRANSFORMED MY LIFE DEEPLY:

Reconnecting to myself, being in touch with my essence, passion, and living to a purpose bigger than myself, allowed me to become the author of my story:

That's because I brought my purpose and my passion to the world - my greatest gifts - in the greatest service to the world: that's when the light of being WHO I TRULY AM started to reverberate - that's both the purpose and the fulfillment of our inner journey.

That well-being leads to inspiration, which becomes the fuel for creating different things and even more fulfillment - that's why I call it EXPONENTIAL FULFILLMENT.

When I lived like a zombie, all I wanted was to have a fairy godmother to sparkle some clarity of mind about myself and my purpose to help me feel alive again.

If this resonates with you, I'd love to spark that clarity, help you improve the relationship with yourself, and honor your mighty life purpose.

Which kinda begs the question: What fires you up?

Please, let me know if you have any questions:

info@daniferrara.com
daniferrara.com

www.ingramcontent.com/pod-product-compliance
Lightning Source LLC
Chambersburg PA
CBHW052335220526
45472CB00001B/427